ART DECO

POSTERS AND GRAPHICS

Robert Bonfils
Exposition Internationale des Arts Décoratifs et Industriels Modernes, 1925

ART DECO
POSTERS AND GRAPHICS

Jean Delhaye

ACADEMY EDITIONS · LONDON/ST. MARTIN'S PRESS · NEW YORK

ACKNOWLEDGEMENTS

We would like to thank the Victoria and Albert Museum for permission to photograph works in their collection which appear on the frontispiece and pages 6,7,15,19,50 (top), 76,77,89 and 95; and Mr. James Wormser for providing the transparency of the poster in his collection illustrated on p 47. We are particularly indebted to Victor Arwas and Editions Graphiques gallery for permission to photograph works in their possession from which the majority of the remaining illustrations are reproduced.

Title page illustration:
Jacques Darcy
Parfum Shalimar, 1928

INTRODUCTION

'Have you ever considered how sad streets, squares, railway stations, underground stations, grand hotels, nightclubs, cinemas, dining-cars, travel, highways, nature, would be without those innumerable posters, without window displays (those lovely new toys for thoughtful families); without the chat from loudspeakers; and can you conceive how sad and dull would be meals without multicoloured menus and pretty labels?' wrote the French poet and novelist Blaise Cendrars in 1927. 'That which characterises the whole of the world's advertising is its lyricism.' And thinking of Cassandre he added: 'And here advertising approaches poetry.' Such words echo curiously in an era which agitates for the abolition of excess advertising, where the bemused driver on some highway can drive for miles and see little but advertising, and question, with Ogden Nash, if he has ever seen 'a billboard pretty as a tree.'

The innocent days of the Art Nouveau poster did not long outlive the turn of the century. It was no longer enough to have a pretty lady with long hair, or a finely decorative composition, dramatically angled for its artistic effect: the poster had to be commercially successful in its ability to sell not itself, but the product it advertised.

Leonetto Cappiello (1875–1942), born in Livorno in Italy, arrived in Paris in 1898, and became an instant success as a humorous cartoonist, and his albums of caricatures, particularly those of famous actresses, were enormously successful. In 1899 he produced his first poster then, from 1904 onwards, was to devote himself to the poster, with only the occasional decorative composition or book illustration to distract him: he was to produce over three thousand posters. Clearly influenced by Chéret, Cappiello was first to realise that the poster needed instant impact, and needed to attract the attention not only of the stroller who could stop by, say, a low-hung Mucha poster and spend some time admiring its intricate line and subtle colour harmonies, but

also of the busy person hurrying by in carriage or car. His posters became larger, occupying high and wide vantage points. There was little point in subtlety there, the composition needed to be simplified and strongly coloured, the message clear and simple. When composing a poster, he said, one must relate all its different parts into a single effective structure, which he called the arabesque. The poster's arabesque was the graphic expression of its slogan, message or label: needing to be seen clearly, its meaning or symbolism grasped quickly and its shape retained in the mind. 'C'est l'arabesque qui attire, qui retient, qui subsiste' ('It is the arabesque which attracts, detains, survives'), he wrote. Cappiello's characters are nearly all in constant movement. They ride, dance, prance in flaming colour contrasts. Some of his images, like the 1909 Thermogène Pierrot clutching the warming cotton-wool pads to his chest and blowing flames from his mouth, were to be used for over fifty years, and became part of the environment for several generations in France and elsewhere. He remained faithful to his basic formula throughout his posters, devising memorable characters or images which remained linked to the product that had inspired them.

The various events and movements which had stunned and shaken the art establishment in the early days of the century quickly filtered into the world of advertising. Cubism, Futurism, Fauvism, and the oriental opulence of the Ballets Russes, all helped give the poster artist a wider range of potential colours and images. And in their turn posters using colours and images derived from these movements, in however debased a form, enabled the public to become used to the *look* of the avant garde and, by extension, prepared the public, or some of it, to accept the real thing. The reverse of the coin was that the public became used to novelty, inured to its impact, and impatient for greater visual thrills. The street was the

5

Charles Loupot
Exposition Internationale des Arts Décoratifs et Industriels Modernes, 1925

average man's art gallery. Cassandre, according to Blaise Cendrars, was the street's first stage director.

Born in Kharkov, in the Ukraine, of French parents, Adolphe Jean-Marie Mouron (1901–1968) had studied in Paris at some of the finest ateliers, notably the Grande Chaumière, the Académie Julian, and the studios of the idealist painter René Ménard and the realist Lucien Simon. In 1924 he produced his first poster, *Bucheron,* for a furniture maker. This poster was signed 'Cassandre', adopting the name of Troy's doom-laden prophetess, but his later posters were usually signed 'A. M. Cassandre', using the initials of his real name. His *Pivolo* poster of 1924 and the extraordinary *L'Intransigeant* poster of 1925, in which the newsvendor's face is simplified to a cut-out outline, the newspaper's title being chopped to its popular contraction 'L'Intrans', won him the Grand Prix for posters at the 1925 Paris International Exhibition of Decorative and Industrial Arts, the exhibition which gave its name to Art Deco.

In 1926 Cassandre met the young Maurice A. Moyrand. Together with another poster artist, Loupot, they founded a new advertising agency, the Alliance Graphique, run adventurously by Moyrand, and for which Cassandre produced a run of highly individual posters between 1927 and 1934. Unlike Cappiello's posters, Cassandre's reveal no basic formula. Each uses an essentially schematic form to illuminate product or slogan, simplifying, superimposing, adopting cubist analysis, photography, collage or distortion for effect, but always providing the unexpected illustration. He was wont to point out that the commercial poster was made to be seen and noted by people who were not looking, who lived in the midst of a visual uproar in which an individual image struck only like an optical accident. This poster penetrated one's sensibilities 'not like an easel painter, through the door like a gentleman; but like a burglar, through the window, holding a jemmy.'

The role of the poster artist was clearly defined by Cassandre: 'The poster demands complete renunciation from its painter. He *cannot* express himself in it. Were he able to, he would not have the right. Painting is an end in itself. The poster is only a means, a means of communication between tradesman and public, something like the telegraph. The poster artist plays the part of the telegraphist: he does not *emit* messages, he *transmits* them. One does not ask him for his advice, one merely asks him to establish clear, powerful and precise communication.'

Cassandre produced clear, powerful posters for French and British firms until 1934, when his friend Moyrand died, many inspired by the aerodynamic lines of large-scale transport, ships and railways. From then on he only very occasionally produced a poster, concentrating on designing several new printer's type-faces. In 1936 he travelled to the United States, where he produced a number of illustrations for *Harper's Bazaar* over a three year period. On his return to France he spent the rest of his life working on theatrical design.

Charles Loupot (1892–1971), Cassandre's fellow artist in the Alliance Graphique, had begun as an illustrator for the fashion-plate magazine, the *Gazette du Bon-Ton* (The Good Taste Gazette). His first posters were entirely in the somewhat mannered transitional style favoured by the magazine and, indeed, he occasionally returned to the style in his later posters. Yet most of the posters he produced in his Alliance Graphique days were highly stylised. He continued to produce posters after the war. Pierre-Felix Fix-Masseau (1869–1937) who, in the latter days of the nineteenth century had been a fine Art Nouveau sculptor, producing at least one superb Symbolist bronze, turned to poster design in the inter-war years, rivalling Cassandre in the production of hieratic images for ships and trains.

Jean Carlu (b. 1900) was, with Cassandre, one of the great innovators of the poster, using the language of Cubism in conjunction with every available new technique, including photography. He pioneered the coloured neon-tube poster, both as actuality and as reproduced on paper, and produced a number of vast three-dimensional posters using stove-enamelled metal sheets in combination with neon tubes bent into the appropriate shapes to produce coloured lines. Carlu was in the United States when the Second World War broke out, and he there executed many posters, winning a contest for the best poster to help the war effort. He returned to France after the war, and created many well-known images.

Paul Colin (b. 1892) came to Paris from his native Nancy, and was chosen by Rolf de Maré in 1923 to become principal stage designer and poster artist for the new Théâtre des Champs Elysées. Colin's best posters were inspired by the stage, his style being somewhat more conventional than that of Carlu or Cassandre, but with a cheerful grotesquerie in the treatment of characters which was both powerful and memorable. His poster for the *Revue Nègre* and others for Joséphine Baker are indelibly a part of the visual landscape of that era.

Colin was, however, an exception among theatre poster artists in the degree of freedom he was allowed. The caricatural element was always strong in such posters, yet it was also essential not to harm the artistes involved by ridiculing them. The fine line was trodden sure-footedly by Kiffer in his Maurice Chevalier posters, all grin and panama hat, or Arton Girbal in his for the monumentally red-haired Gaby Montbreuse. The great Mistinguett appeared almost unrecognizably in Cappiello's 1920 poster for the Casino de Paris, but her very own favourite, almost exclusive artist, was Charles Gesmar (1900–1928), a very young man who, in his brief life helped define her persona by designing stunningly befeathered exotic costumes for her, as well as appropriate sets and large posters in which her impish smile overwhelms the spectator. Gesmar

Leonetto Cappiello
'*Délices*', 1923

had joined the Casino de Paris shortly after his seventeenth birthday, designing Miss' costumes for the 1918 show, *Pa-ri-ki-ri* (Laughing Paris) in which she and Maurice Chevalier were appearing. He became so attached to her that he was called 'Maman' (Mother) by everyone at the theatre.

After Gesmar's death several of the Casino de Paris' designers produced posters for Miss, but the most striking are undoubtedly those produced in the late twenties and early thirties by Zig (whose real name was Brummer) who also produced exciting posters for other stars of the theatre and music-hall, notably Joséphine Baker.

The inter-war years saw a wide gap developing between 'Commercial' artists, specialising in posters, and 'serious' artists. It was acceptable for the 'serious' easel painter to occasionally illustrate books or produce some original lithographs or etchings, but few considered the poster worth tackling. Kees Van Dongen

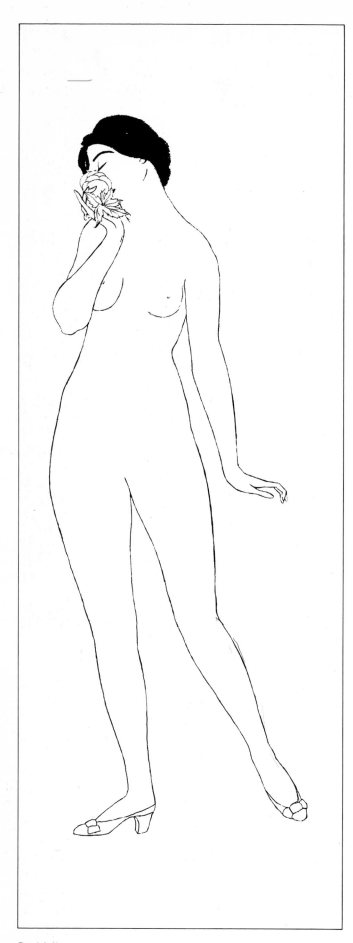

Paul Iribe
La Rose, 1912

(1877–1968) was one of the few. Exhibiting his paintings with the Fauves group, he soon showed both an independence of, and a disregard for, the snobbish conventions of art critics to become a fashionable portrait painter, clearly enjoying both the notoriety and the rewards. He illustrated several books with masterly brio, and even turned his hand to the straightforward commercial poster.

Jean Gabriel Domergue (1889–1964), an equally fashionable painter and creator of a long-limbed, long necked, elegant creature who became the epitome of the Parisienne, also occasionally produced posters for some seaside resorts, the occasional theatrical act, or charity ball. Unlike Van Dongen, who created his posters as individual responses to the product advertised, Domergue generally illustrated a single central figure which was characteristic of his own work.

Marcel Vertes (1895–1962), a Hungarian, had become one of the leading poster artists in Vienna in the early twenties before arriving in Paris. In 1925 he produced two albums, *Dancings,* a set of colour lithographs which illustrated the humorous, sad, exhilarating, absurd, aspects of night life in Paris: and *Maisons,* a set of black-and-white lithographs dealing with the delights on offer in the bordellos of Paris. In the years that followed, Vertes executed a variety of book illustrations, drawings, paintings and murals that constantly explored the twin veins of night life. He only rarely produced posters in France, generally for charity balls and other social events.

Cubism as such was too rigorous and dry an art form to touch the great public. The new vision of Cubism, however, developed into a geometrism of line which was absorbed by artists at every level, and popularised in the fashionable pursuits; stage and costume designs, drawings for fashion and society magazines, fabrics and book illustrations. Artists like Robert Bonfils (1886–1971), Guy Arnoux (d. 1951), François-Louis Schmied (1873–1941), and Georges Barbier (1882–1932), designed and illustrated a variety of books and other publications, in which the images, frequently in colour, gave a richness to the whole which was balanced by adventurous type-faces and layouts. Raoul Dufy (1877–1953) produced a series of large woodcuts which were used as designs for fabrics by Bianchini-Ferrier; Jean-Emile Laboureur (1877–1943) developed a 'popular' variety of Cubism in his etchings, which followed his fine sturdy woodcuts; Tsougouharu Foujita (1886–1968) used his sharp Japanese vision to produce ravishing images of the Parisian

8

woman; Marie Laurencin illustrated books and produced the occasional poster; Robert (1885–1941) and Sonia Delauney (1885–) developed their theories of simultaneity, he in his paintings and lithographs, she also in her coordinated designs for fabrics, furs, clothes and even cars. Art Deco was being created. The 1925 Paris International Exhibition was the great showcase for all the innovations that had taken place in the previous quarter century. Established artists like Paul Iribe (1883–1935), Georges Barbier, Georges Lepape (1887–1971) or Garcia Benito (b.1892), who had simplified line with a touch of romance in such fashion magazines as the *Gazette du Bon-Ton*, reached the height of their fame and glory then.

One important by-way of Art Deco imagery was the animalier movement. Heirs of a tradition that has lasted as long as there have been animals and people who paint, draw or sculpt, the Art Deco animaliers succeeded in recreating the tradition, rejecting absolute realism in favour of stylisation, yet at the same time maintaining a realistic integrity which allowed the animals depicted all of their dignity and might. All the felines appear, cats as well as lions and tigers, panthers, leopards and jaguars; elephants, both wild and domesticated, often appear; snakes made magnificent decorative patterns; and so did birds of prey.

The most consistently original animalier graphic artist was Paul Jouve (1880–). Son of a portrait painter, Jouve first exhibited some drawings and lithographs of Abyssinian lions at the age of fifteen at the Salon of the Société Nationale des Beaux-Arts. Three years later he sculpted a frieze of stylised animals which was made in ceramic by Bigot. One hundred metres long, the frieze was part of the monumental gate designed by the architect René Binet for the 1900 Paris Universal Exhibition. Long visits to the zoos of Antwerp and Hamburg were followed, in 1904, by a three-year trip to Algeria paid for by a scholarship from the Society of French Orientalists. More study visits to the zoos of Europe were followed by a major commission from a group of bibliophiles to illustrate Kipling's *The Jungle Book*. The book was to take some ten years to prepare. Jouve produced a vast number of finished drawings which were then cut on wood by F. L. Schmied. The book was finally published in 1920 in an edition of only 125 copies. In the meantime, Jouve had gone to Cambodia, where he executed drawings which eventually led to his illustrations of Pierre Loti's book *Le Pélerin d'Angkor* (The Pilgrim from Angkor), once again engraved on

Georges Barbier
Thamar Karsavina

wood by F. L. Schmied. Of the many animalier etchings Jouve was to produce, one of his most striking sets was *Dix Eaux-Fortes Originales et Un Frontispice*, luxuriously cased in a brass studded pigskin binder executed by Hermès.

Another powerful set of illustrations for *The Jungle Book* was produced by Henri Deluermoz. Born in Paris in 1876 Deluermoz studied with Gustave Moreau and A. P. Roll. He was a figure and landscape painter, but principally an animalier, exhibiting at the Salon of the Société Nationale des Beaux-Arts, of which he was both an elected member and on its Executive; and contributing to the exhibitions of the Society of French Animalier Painters, of which he was also a member; as well as holding several one-man shows in commercial galleries, notably in 1913,

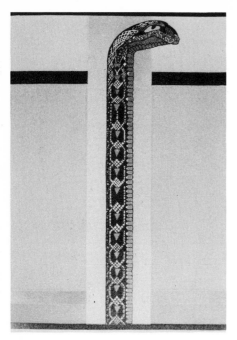

François-Louis Schmied
Salammbô — Serpent, 1923

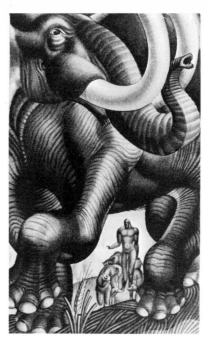

Andre Durenceau
Eléphant, 1932

François-Louis Schmied
Illustration

1919 and 1927. To illustrate Kipling he produced a large number of watercolours and gouaches, paintings and monotypes in muted shades of sepia and brown, several heightened with gold, the whole effect being one seemingly inspired by lacquerwork. These designs were then engraved on wood by Théo Schmied, F. L. Schmied's son. This enterprise, too, took many years of preparation before being eventually published in January 1941 in an edition of 250 copies.

François-Louis Schmied was born in Geneva, and studied wood-engraving there at the School of Industrial Arts, where he and Jean Dunand, who was studying sculpture, became friends. In 1895 Schmied joined Dunand in Paris, and found great difficulty in obtaining work. Jouve had seen some of Schmied's work, and he insisted on employing him to transfer his watercolours and drawings onto wood for *The Jungle Book.* Schmied began the wood-engravings in 1910, printing a few proofs in colour of each block as he went on, but the outbreak of war in 1914 was to interrupt the work. Schmied, who was a Swiss citizen, enrolled in the French Foreign Legion. Wounded in the battle of the Somme, Schmied lost his right eye, and won both the Military Medal and the Croix-de-Guerre. Invalided out, he resumed work on *The Jungle Book,* which was eventually published in 1920. Schmied's skill, subtlety and interpretative skill was clearly evident, his reputation assured. In the years that followed he was to control almost every aspect of

the books he worked on, illustration, choice of text, layout, typography and printing, frequently acting as his own publisher, and even designing and occasionally executing his own bindings. He was to form a close knit group with his friends Jean Dunand, Jean Goulden, and Jouve, frequently exhibiting together, often collaborating on the same works, their small group being somewhat expanded by the addition of the sculptor Gustav Miklos and Dunand's son Bernard and Schmied's son Théo. Schmied's own illustrations were often engraved on wood by Théo, or lacquered by Dunand, sometimes coloured by Miklos; he himself frequently engraved or elaborated illustrations by Dunand, Jouve and Miklos. Goulden, who married Schmied's daughter in 1925, was a brilliant enameller, but also wealthy enough to commission works from every member of the group.

Joseph Hecht (1891–1951) was another important animalier artist. Born in Lodz, in Poland, he became a disciple of Stanley William Hayter's in Paris, though he was never to follow Hayter into the realms of abstraction, retaining a firm grasp on reality. He was both painter and graphic artist, specialising in burin engraving, slicing through the metal to obtain a rich black line which was ideal to interpret his almost primitive vision of a paradise in which animals and naked humans lived in harmony. He exhibited in the Paris Salon d'Automme, the Salon des Tuileries and the Salon des Indépendants, as well as holding several one-man exhibitions in Paris, New York, Philadelphia and London.

Certain graphic artists struck a popular vein of Art Deco imagery, the pretty pert Parisienne, often partially undraped, seen against various backgrounds. The antecedents of the image are found in the pages of *La Vie Parisienne* and other similar magazines. The Gibson Girl may well have been her mother. Yet these were not magazine illustrations, confined by definition within the pages of a publication, to be looked at furtively in the privacy of study or bedroom, but large decorative colour etchings and aquatints to be framed and displayed openly in gallery and living room. William Ablett (1878–1936) was one such artist. Born in Paris of British parents, he became a fashionable portrait painter, exhibiting in both Paris and London. He exhibited at the Paris Salon des Artistes Français, where he was awarded an Honourable Mention in 1900, before switching to the Salon of the Société Nationale des Beaux-Arts. In 1909 he was awarded a Silver Medal at the Liège (Belgium) International Exhibition. In London he exhibited at the Royal Academy and the New Gallery, while several of his works went to the United States. In the 1920s and 1930s Ablett, a skilled etcher, produced a number of detailed interior scenes graced with young, attractive, modern women, the whole in colour aquatint. Other artists working in this vein included Kaby, Pisis, Micao Kono and Maurice Millière (b.1871), a prominent portrait and scene painter who exhibited at the Salons of the Société des Artistes Français, of the Société Coloniale des Artistes Français, and of the Humoristes, receiving a Gold Medal at the 1932 Paris Colonial Exhibition. He illustrated several books, and contributed to *La Vie Parisienne,* the *Illustrated London News* and the *North American,* creating a deliciously chubby Parisienne type, with curly hair and cheerful disposition, born around the turn of the century to look a little like a beauty by Helleu, then adapting her in both facial characteristics and makeup to the Edwardian period, the war years, the twenties and the thirties.

Millière had only one serious rival who succeeded in adapting his creations to the changing requirements of fashion over a long period, but this rival was the most famous of them all, Louis Icart (1889–1950). A pre-Great War apprenticeship as a fashion illustrator enabled Icart to study etching techniques. These he put into practice during the war when he produced an album of etchings in colour depicting women's roles while men were out fighting as, indeed, he was himself.

Paul Véra
Nu

He also produced etchings depicting a girl wrapped in the flag of each of the allies, as well as some of allegorical women in bombed-out buildings or in the trenches, bending over dead soldiers or protecting children from the enemy's guns. Icart had found the formula that was to make him enormously successful in the inter-war years. Series of indoor and outdoors girls followed, based on legends, operas, great loves, famous monuments, pets, music hall and concert, boudoir and harem. He devised the aerodynamic girl racing forward with her greyhounds, Leda in the arms of the black swan, and the sensuous semi-clad nymph lolling on a divan, smoking, images which were to become almost clichés of the period. He exhibited at the Salon des Humoristes, but his popularity abroad was such that a Louis Icart Society was formed in New York to distribute his etchings in colour, which were produced in vast numbers. His girls adapted to the changing fashions of the thirties but, after the interruption of the Second World War, he was unable to create a type that could appeal to the public of the late 1940s. He died in 1950 a completely forgotten man, his etchings

Elmer O. Tetzlaff
Dessin d'affiche, 1929

selling, if at all, for pennies until the return of the nostalgia boom in the late 1960s, since when Icart etchings have become more popular and sought after than they had ever been, some attaining phenomenal prices, especially in the United States.

Paul Jacoulet (1902–1960) is in a class by himself. Born in Paris, he was taken to Japan at the age of four, as his father was teaching at the Imperial University in Tokyo: he was to spend the rest of his life in the Far East. He learned Japanese at School, and became adept at its calligraphy with the brush. He also studied painting and drawing, both Eastern and Western, and began collecting Ukiyo-e woodcuts, the images of the 'floating world' of pleasure. Years as an interpreter at the French Embassy and private tutoring alternated with travel throughout the South Sea Islands, the Carolines, the Marshalls, the Marianas, the Celebes, as well as to Korea, Manchuria, Guam. His first exhibition of paintings and drawings was held in Tokyo in 1934, after which he turned to his own version of the Ukiyo-e woodblock print. Working closely with his carvers and printers, he devised more and more complex prints using on occasion up to three hundred

blocks for a single colour woodcut. The paper he used was made especially for him, he mixed his own pigments, often using powdered gold, silver and platinum, pearl, mother-of-pearl, mica and eggshell, and occasionally used embossing and lacquer to obtain certain effects. Most of his subjects record the exotic world of the Far East in all its aspects, much of it vanishing as he recorded it. The Parisienne illustrated here is the only wood-block of a European subject that he produced. All Jacoulet's prints were produced in series for subscribers. This one, dating from 1934, was in a series marked with a Fan Seal.

The years that followed the 1925 Exhibition saw a curious change. While architecture was becoming more functional under the aegis of Le Corbusier and Mallet-Stevens, furniture and artifacts becoming chunkier in the Modernist vein, the cubist-inspired spiky line of Art Deco was giving way to a volumetric neo-classicism that was derived from Ingres, but tended to mythological subjects or allegories, the Seasons, or Peace, or Glory. Artists like Jean Dupas (b.1882), Eugène Pougheon (1886–1955) and Raphael Delorme had created the style with delicacy and panache. The years that followed saw its vulgarisation as it was adapted by the Soviet Union, Italy and Germany as a perfect vehicle for displaying their ideological concepts. Ill served by a succession of uninspired hacks, damned as Fascist art, the early works in the neo-classic style of the twenties and thirties still have many splendid images worth seeking out.

In Germany Lucian Bernhard (1883–1972) broke away from the Jugendstil tradition as early as 1903, simplifying design to a single character or representation of the goods advertised, his forte being his ability to draw original and appropriate lettering. Bernhard produced a vast number of posters consisting of lettering only, or lettering in conjunction with a small device or illustration, succeeding in adapting the form, shape and style of his letters to whatever he was advertising and whatever period he was advertising it in.

The master of the pictorial poster in Germany was, however, Ludwig Hohlwein (1874–1949). Born in Wiesbaden, he studied at the Higher Technical School in Munich before moving to Dresden, and devoted most of his life from 1906 onwards to the poster. Clearly influenced by Charles Rennie Mackintosh and the Beggarstaff Brothers, he developed a powerful style of his own which was clear and colourful, stylised and effective. With great economy of means, he

Louis-Joseph Soulas
Vichy

composes his posters using a powerfully outlined realism which is just sufficiently stylised for effect: the lettering is laid out clearly, placed in blocks when there is a lot of it so that it never fights with the image for attention, but is clearly readable. He only occasionally uses much colour, his poster having one dominant colour over a muted pallette for the rest.

The power of colour had been demonstrated in 1911 by Albert Weisgerber (1878–1915). Born in St. Ingbert, near Saarbrucken, he had been a pupil of Franz Von Stuck before joining him in the new Munich Secession. He produced some fine posters, notably for the 1910 Brussels International Exhibition, in which a nude male figure creates a whirl of colour by waving and intertwining the flags of the participating nations. His finest creation came, however, the following year, when he designed a poster for a Munich restaurant for artists and students, *Der Bunte Vogel,* in which a

toucan and some wine bottles create an image both strong and memorable with an exciting juxtaposition of colours each of which is strong enough not to have to fight for attention. The image of the toucan was later adopted in Britain in a long and famous advertising campaign for Guinness Stout.

Hans Rudi Erdt (1883–c1918) also studied in Munich, but moved to Berlin in 1908, where he produced a succession of striking posters for theatre, exhibitions, newspapers, films, cars and cigarettes, frequently using as motifs the well-dressed man and woman about town. Like Weisgerber, who was killed at Yprès, Erdt did not survive the Great War of 1914–1918. Jupp Wiertz (1888–1939), born at Aix-la-Chapelle, died in Berlin shortly after the start of the Second World War. He had studied at the School of Decorative Arts in Berlin and became one of Germany's leading poster artists in the inter-war years,

Albert Weisgerber
Der Bunte Vogel, 1911

producing a succession of impressive images for theatre, magazines and tourism, though his three most striking images are the deliciously greedy, befeathered and elegant young woman dipping into her box of Riquet pralines; the equally delicious beauty with her Japanese parasol for Kaloderma soap; and the retrospectively sinister image of a zeppelin bearing a swastika moored to a New York skyscraper, designed to advertise transatlantic travel by the airship.

The German cinema was, until the coming to power of the Nazi Party, one of the freest and most adventurous in the world. Fritz Lang's *Metropolis* (1919) had, in its powerful settings, set the standard for all subsequent science-fiction-cum-disaster movies; Murnau's *Nosferatu* set a pattern for later horror films; *The Cabinet of Dr. Caligari* was an extraordinary essay into

psychological disorientation through the use of expressionist sets and stylised acting. Yet apart from these exceptional films, the studios churned out hundreds of films every year, including comedies, love stories, mysteries, spectaculars and erotic tales. As is only to be expected, the majority of such posters were hurriedly put together as basic exploitation material, and are often repetitive and rarely creative. Nevertheless a number of excellent poster artists produced some very fine ones for the movies, including Ludwig Kainer (b.1885), Karl Michel (b.1885), Ludwig Hohlwein, the Austrian Julius Klinger (b.1876) and Julius Gipkens (b.1883). The German cinema, however, found one great artist devoted to it: Joseph Fennecker (1895–1956). Born at Bocholt in Westphalia Fennecker studied in Münster, Dusseldorf and Munich and was a pupil of Emil Orlik in Berlin. Interested in the theatre, he designed sets for productions all over Europe, yet spent much of his life working for the cinema. His first movie posters date from 1918, when he designed for a series of Berlin cinemas, but he designed exclusively for the Marmorhaus (Marble House) Cinema in Berlin from 1919 to 1924. He contributed to such publications as *Simplicissimus, Jugend* and fashion magazines, later working more for the theatre and opera. His 1921 poster for the Berlin Luna-Park is as gay and cheerful as some of his posters for Asta Nielsen are tragic.

The Italian poster in the inter-war years was largely dominated by the figure of Marcello Dudovich (1878–1962). Born in Trieste, Dudovich joined the Milan firm of Ricordi as a lithographer. Working under the poster designer Leopoldo Metlicovitz, he soon became an excellent designer as well as executant. After leaving Ricordi he joined the printing firm of Chapuis in Bologna, and there met painters, composers and writers. His posters won him a Gold Medal at the Paris Universal Exhibition in 1900. He rejoined the Ricordi firm, the major advertising agency and poster publisher in Italy, in 1905. He continued to draw and paint, contributing mostly fashion illustrations to the Munich magazine *Simplicissimus,* while continuing to create fine and original posters, largely on fashion themes, including a famous series for the Milan department store *La Rinascente.* There were, of course, many other fine graphic designers, among whom may be mentioned Sergio Tofano, who signed himself 'Sto', Federico Seneca, Codognato Plinio and L.A. Mauzan.

When one considers the vast potential of

advertising in the United States, it is amazing how few original posters were produced in the Art Deco style. The Art Nouveau movement had produced a fine group of poster artists there. The inter-war years saw a proliferation of a type of rustic, home-spun illustration outside the scope of this volume. Much of the advertising was designed for readability and impact, but tended to use photographic blow-ups rather than drawn images. When advertisers sought drawn images, they tended to turn to French or other European artists. A somewhat Art Deco tradition is, however, found in some illustrators, for instance John Held Jr (1889–1958), Rockwell Kent (1882–1971) and John Vassos (b.1898).

Curiously enough, the leading designer of Art Deco posters in Great Britain was an American, Edward McKnight Kauffer (1890–1954). Born in Great Falls, Montana, he was educated in Indiana, and arrived in Europe at the age of twenty-two. He executed his first London Transport poster in 1915, then went on to create memorable images for some forty years, many for London Transport, Shell Oil, and Imperial Airways. In fact, London Transport was a great patron of poster artists, though most fall outside the scope of this volume, while several of those that could be called Art Deco were executed by Jean Dupas.

The boom in etchings in the inter-war years in Britain had almost no connection with Art Deco. Some etchings and drypoints by Lettice Sanford, Robert S. Austin (1895–1973), William E. C. Morgan (b.1903), E. H. Lacey (b. 1892) and John Buckland-Wright are clearly within that movement by their sharp and simple linear treatment of characteristic images. Many of Sir William Russell Flint's (1880–1969) fine drypoints and a few of the highly elaborate stipple etchings of Gerald Leslie Brockhurst (b. 1890) also stem from a similar inspiration. Book illustrators such as John Austen, Beresford Egan and the Australian Norman Lindsay transformed the line bequeathed to them by Aubrey Beardsley into personal arabesques which form about the only original British contribution to the Art Deco image. Parallel with these are the book illustrations of Vera Willoughby, Edmund Dulac (1882–1953) and Kay Nielsen (1886–1957) whose work was entirely within the French tradition.

The Art Deco image is clearly less homogeneous than the Art Nouveau one, encompassing as

Edward McKnight Kauffer
Daily Herald — The Early Bird, 1919

it does the elegant Parisienne, the caricatured star, the boudoir baby, Ballets Russes opulence, Cubist lines, photographic collage, neo-classical massiveness of volume and geometric simplification. Yet it is always clearly recognisable because of the style, stylisation and stylishness that bring unity to its diversity.

A.M. Cassandre
Nord-Express, 1927

A.M. Cassandre
Etoile du Nord, 1927

Jean Carlu
Pépa Bonafé, 1928

Paul Colin
Wiener & Doucet

Paul Colin
Joséphine Baker

Paul Colin
Joséphine Baker

Paul Colin
Tabarin, 1928

Kees van Dongen
Les Cheveux courts

André Lhote
Nu sur un divan

Ludwig Hohlwein
Damenstrumpfe Marke

Marie Laurencin
Gravures, 1937

Paul Iribe
La Morte de Circé — Art moderne, 1928

Paul Iribe
La Morte de Circé — Tableau cubiste, 1928

Jean-Emile Laboureur
Architectures – Le Kiosque à journaux, 1921

Guy Arnoux
Les Femmes de ce temps — La Danseuse éperdue, 1920

Guy Arnoux
Les Femmes de ce temps — L'Indifférente, 1920

Guy Arnoux
Les Femmes de ce temps — L'Etrange, 1920

Edouard Chimot
La Petite Jeanne pâle, 1922

Marcel Vertès
Dancings — Le Jazz, 1925

Marcel Vertès
Dancings — Le Réveillon, 1925

Franz Masereel
Die Stadt, 1925

Franz Masereel
Die Stadt, 1925

Page 34 — Wilhelm Harz
Da Capo

Da Capo

Trustfreie Qualitäts - Cigarette

Zig (Brummer)
Casino de Paris: Mistinguett, 1931

Page 36 — Zig (Brummer)
Casino de Paris: Mistinguett, 1930

Zig (Brummer)
Joséphine Baker au Casino de Paris, 1930

Georges Lepape
Poiret le magnifique

Georges Lepape
Dress Silks, 1928

Paul Jouve
Panthère

Paul Jouve
Aigle

Joseph Hecht
Eléphants

Paul Jouve
Léopard

Paul Iribe
Jeanne Lanvin et sa fille

François-Louis Schmied
Repos

François-Louis Schmied
Illustration

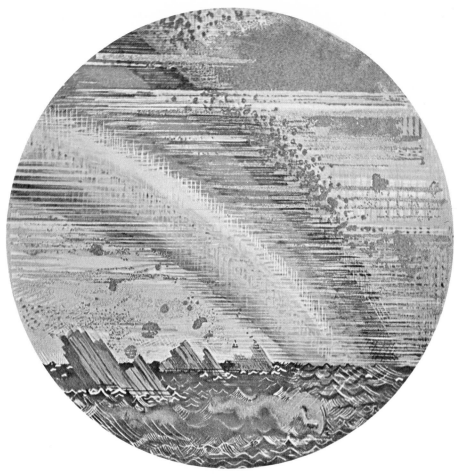

François-Louis Schmied
La Légende du martin-pêcheur, c. 1926

Henri Deluermoz
Le Livre de la Jungle: Panthère

Arton Girbal
Gaby Montbreuse, 1924

Charles Gesmar
Mistinguett, 1925

Guy Sabran
Illustration

Guy Sabran
Illustration

René Vincent
Peugeot

Anderson
Shell, 1935

E. Roowy
Pneu Pirelli

Ah !........ si vous aviez une
Peugeot

M.S.
Peugeot

Artiste anonyme
Voisin Automobiles

Automne

HISPANO SUIZA

Magasin d'Exposition : 150, Avenue des Champs-Elysées — Téléphone : Elysées 55-02

René Ravo
Hispano Suiza

Julius Ussy Engelhard
Klida, 1927

Técla

10 RUE DE LA PAIX, PARIS
7 OLD BOND STREET, LONDRES
398 FIFTH AVENUE, NEW-YORK

EX
Técla

Georges Barbier
Nijinsky, 1912

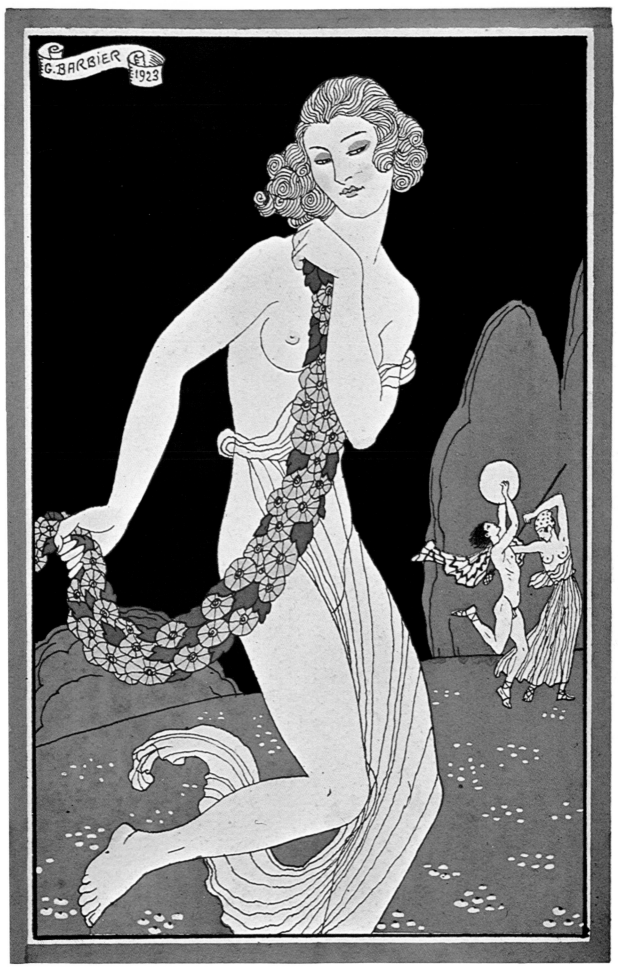

Georges Barbier
Proserpine, 1923

Georges Barbier
Les Chansons de Bilitis, c. 1922

Georges Barbier
Nijinsky, 1913

Louis Icart
Au bar

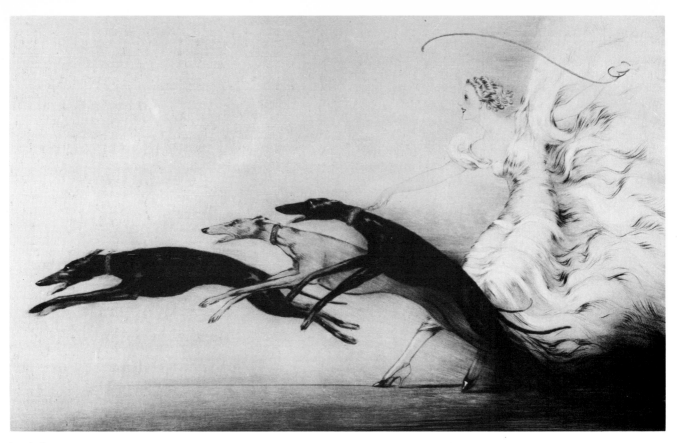

Louis Icart
Vitesse, 1933

Louis Icart
La Grappe de raisins

PÉTROLE HAHN

Contre la chute des cheveux et les pellicules. Assouplit et lustre les cheveux sans graisser. Facilite la coiffure, l'ondulation au fer et la mise en plis sur "indéfrisable". - EN VENTE PARTOUT

Artiste anonyme
Pétrole Hahn

Tsougouharu Foujita
Les Amies

Tsougouharu Foujita
Les Amies II

Tsougouharu Foujita
Parfum Isabey, 1928

Charles Martin
La Gazette du Bon Ton — La Morte d'amour

Paul Chambry
Les Objets d'art, 1927

S. Hruby
Carnaval à Venise à l'Amour, 1922

S. Hruby
Carnaval à Venise au Perroquet, 1922

Edouard Halouze
A. Janesich, 1920

Edouard Halouze
Le Goûter sur la terrasse, 1920

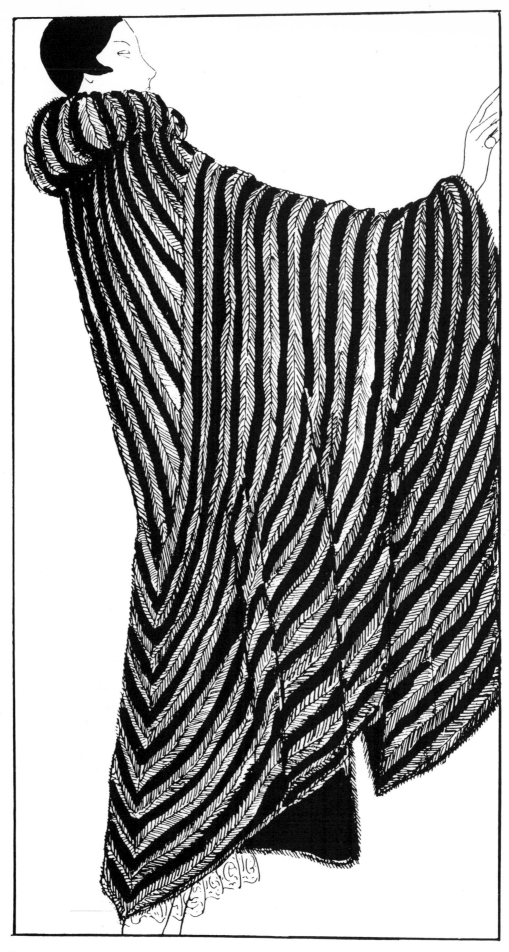

Dartey
Dessin de mode

Dartey
Dessin de mode

Réthaber
Técla

Robert Bonfils
Beaulieu dans les fleurs

Marcel Vertès
Le Tango, 1925

Jean Dupas
London Underground Railway

Jean-Gabriel Domergue
Le Miroir, 1921

Jean-Gabriel Domergue
Aux courses

Alastair (Hans Henning, Baron Voigt)
The Sphinx — Front Decoration, 1920

Within the illustration:

VERLAINE

MODES
LINGERIE
BIBELOTS

16 rue de la PAIX

SIMEON

Siméon
Verlaine

Etienne Drian
Etude, c. 1936

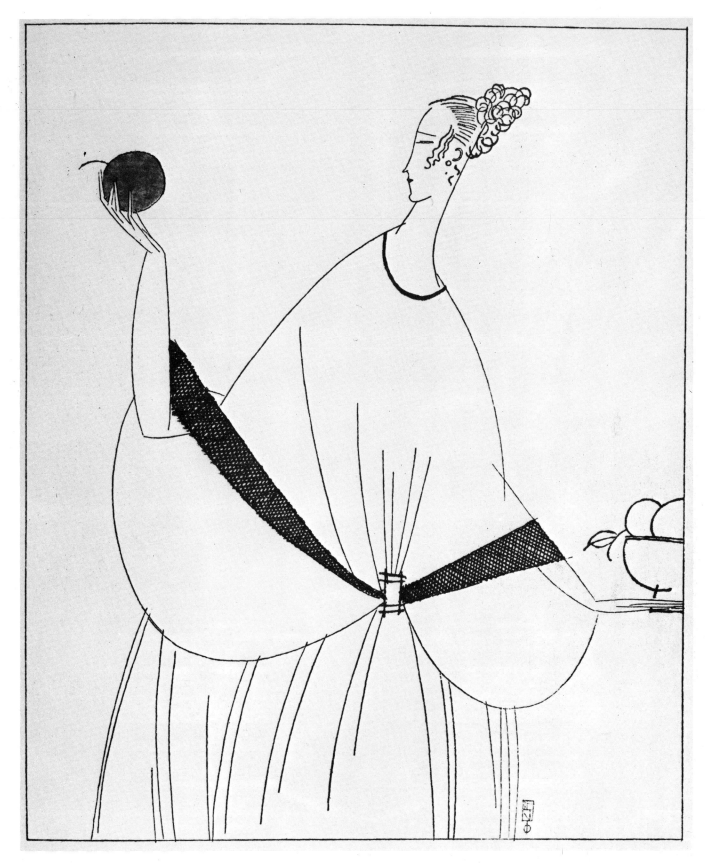

Edouard Garcia Benito
Dessin de mode

Edouard Garcia Benito
Le Boeuf sur le toit

Garcia Benito
La Gazette du Bon Ton: illustration, 1919

Georges Lepape
Bal de la Couture, 1925

M. Gerard
Illustration

Charles Martin
Illustration

EXHIBITION

LA GAZETTE DV BON TON

(HEINEMANN.)

Masterpieces by

BAKST, DRIAN, LEPAPE, MARTY, BRISSDAU, BARBIER ETC.

AT THE FINE ART SOCIETY
148, NEW BOND STREET, W.

Charles Martin
La Gazette du Bon Ton Exhibition

Beresford Egan
Cyprian Masques — Megilla, 1929

Beresford Egan
Cyprian Masques — The Night, 1929

Julius Klinger
Sodom — Prolog, 1909

Julius Klinger
Sodom — Vierter Akt, 1909

John Austen
Everyman & Other Plays — Beauty goeth fast away, 1925

Batty
The Return of Persephone, 1933

INDEX